Dog B

MW01289591

What You Need to Know to Successfully Choose the Right Dog Breed, Raise Them, Care for Them and Also Make Money at The End of it All as a Dog Breeder

By Norman Thornton

Contents

Thank you for buying this book and I hope that you will find it useful. If you will want to share your thoughts on this book, you can do so by leaving a review on the Amazon page, it helps me out a lot.

Introduction: Choosing To Breed

Coming to be a dog breeder is never ever a thing that you ought to do gently, and never something that you ought to choose without numerous hours of consideration and preparation. If you are going to be breeding dogs, then there are several things that you ought to think thoroughly about.

Breeding dogs is something that needs a great deal of effort, and something that needs a lifetime dedication on your part. For that reason, if you are going to be breeding dogs, you need to have some significant aspects of your life that focus on dogs.

Firstly, a love for dogs is an excellent start, however it should not be the sole reason why you believe you would be an excellent dog breeder. A love for dogs is really essential due to the fact that you are going to be devoting numerous hours of each of your days raising pups, dealing with your dogs, and making certain that they are healthy. Adoring them is necessary, yes, however adoring them is not the only thing that is necessary, due to the fact that simply love alone can just get you so far.

Besides adoring your dogs, you are going to want to be a dog person. This is different from caring about dogs. Loving dogs may indicate that you delight in having them, that you maintain them around and take them out when required. Being a dog person is much distinct.

Being a dog person implies that you discover dog hair in your soup and do not mind, and that your dogs typically live more conveniently than you do. If you are a dog person you would never ever imagine enabling your dogs to be out in the cold weather, and you would not ever expect them to reside in conditions that you would not live in on your own.

In case you are a dog person you read all that there is to read about your specific dog breed, and you research all of it to learn the important things that you ought to be doing. A dog person may joke that their life focuses on their dogs, and they are most likely right.

For that reason, in order to be a great breeder, you need to be these things. You need to want to deal with your dog breeds and to ensure that you are performing all that you can to offer dogs with great homes. You should be persistent, and prepared to work for the common good of the dog.

And, the bottom line when it concerns dog breeding is that you must not be in it at all for the cash. The cash must never ever be an inspiration for dog breeding, therefore if this is your primary inspiration, it is time for you to go back and search for another pastime.

Breeders who breed for the cash are never ever going to be excellent breeders. As a matter of fact, a lot of breeders, who are doing it properly, do not make much cash at all, since breeders wind up investing the cash that they do make with pups on items for their dogs, shots, and on the breeding process. For that reason, you must constantly understand that the cash isn't going to be a significant factor in whether your dog breeding achieves success.

There are some questions that you must ask yourself if you intend on breeding. Addressing these questions is a fantastic method to make certain that you are prepared for breeding dogs.

Why am I carrying this out?

Am I attempting to generate income?

Am I prepared to enable dogs to be a huge part of my life?

Will I allow them to sleep in my bed with me?

Do I have a terrific breeding strategy in place?

Do I have assistance and support-- either from individuals near me, or from a source such as a breeding group?

Do I understand how to discover answers to my concerns?

Is there somebody else who can take control of my breeding program in case something should occur to me?

Am I prepared to handle pregnant dogs?

Am I prepared to raise pups by hand?

Can I be responsible for discovering houses for each of the pups I create?

Not just that, but can I be responsible for making certain that the pups I produce do not have young puppies on their own?

Am I prepared to really birth pups?

Can I manage handling ill pups, or puppies that do not make it?

Am I prepared for distress when it comes time to give puppies away, or to deal with pups that simply failed to make it through?

Will I understand how to read my female dog and understand when she's had enough?

Will I have the ability to give up if it simply isn't working for me?

Am I prepared for the happiness that goes along with dog breeding, along with the difficult times?

The responses to these questions will aid you to determine if you are ready to end up being a dog breeder. It is necessary that you ensure you understand the responses before you start.

Chapter 1: Discovering the Right Dog Breed

There are numerous things that you ought to do when you are looking at discovering the appropriate dog breed. It is extremely crucial that you discover the appropriate breed, due to the fact that this is going to be the most effective method for you to be effective at dog breeding.

First off, when you are trying to find the appropriate dog breed, you wish to make sure that you learn as much information about the breeds that you are thinking about as feasible. This information is going to assist you make a great decision when it pertains to the kind of dogs that you wish to breed.

The first thing to consider is whether you wish to breed purebred dogs. This is one thing to think thoroughly about. Some dogs, such as golden retrievers and labs, could be bred with dogs which aren't pedigreed. You may wish to do this due to the fact that you like the kind of dog that you have and due to the fact that you feel that others may like those dogs too. In this case, you 'd be trying to find 2 dogs that you wish to breed, however you would not be as worried about the pedigrees as you would if you were trying to find purebred dogs.

Breeding dogs that aren't purebreds could be extremely tough to do, nevertheless, since you do not have the appropriate information about the dogs and about what they could be like. For that reason, choosing to breed pure-blooded dogs can, in fact, be better since you will have the ability to take a look at their family trees, and ensure that you are breeding a set that is going to produce great puppies.

You likewise wish to think of the sizes of the dogs that you wish to be breeding. You need to be taking a look at a size that clicks with you. Keep in mind that the ideal breeders keep their dogs in the house with them-- breeding dogs must not be kept outdoors and must not be kept in kennels or runs. So, you wish to select a breed that is going to be ideal for your house life. For example, if you have a little home, breeding small dogs is most likely better. In case you have a big house with a great deal of space for larger dogs, you can think about breeding larger dogs.

When you have actually selected a breed of dogs, proceed and do some research so that you can find all of the fine points about the dog that you have actually selected. You wish to take a look at what breeders are presently breeding for with a specific kind of dog, and you wish to see what kinds of things breeders are trying to breed.

Likewise, you'll wish to think of things such as character, and about ensuring that the dogs you are breeding have the appropriate character. Aim to see if the breed is great with kids and other animals.

And listen in on a few of the online discussions regarding breeding your specific kind of dog. You wish to ensure that you are entering into a breeding program that suits your requirements-- and one where individuals are going to be prepared and ready to assist you along a bit. This is really essential due to the fact that it will provide you an opportunity to ensure that you are doing the appropriate thing.

Chapter 2: Making A Breeding Strategy

As you start to breed, you are going to want to have a breeding strategy. This may sound ludicrous, however, it is really essential. A breeding strategy is something that you need to have before you even obtain the dogs that you are intending on breeding.

A breeding strategy needs to be made up of a number of things. To start with, you require an idea of the kind of dog that you are going to be breeding. This consists of the information that you have actually currently found out about the breed that you have actually selected.

Next, you wish to take a look at the breeding requirements for that kind of dog, and find out which of the requirements you are going to be breeding for with the dogs that you are breeding. A great breeder aims to keep the breeding requirements and will attempt to breed those factors into his/her dogs.

Next, you will wish to have a breeding strategy that checks out the numerous manners in which the breeding program is going to be established. Include information about making certain that you have a great questionnaire and a waiting list program, and information about how you intend on screening applications for your pups to pick great homes.

Your breeding strategy must then explain how many dogs you intend on having and where you intend to keep them. If the concept of putting dogs in your yard, or having a shed to keep your dogs even crosses your mind, leave breeding immediately. Your dogs need to remain in your home and need to be a part of your household. This is how you produce excellent pups.

Your breeding strategy ought to consist of the ways in which you are going to handle the dogs that you have in your program. It must have information about the number of dogs you'll have in your house, and how those dogs are going to be trained and taken care of.

Then, include information in your breeding strategy about approximately how many litters you intend on having with the dogs. Remember that you should not breed a female dog every time she enters into season, which suggests that you are going to just have one litter a year, at most, for every female dog that you have in your program. A great breeding outfit is going to focus on this and is not going to breed females in back to back heat cycles.

Your breeding strategy additionally needs to have information about how you plan on keeping your dogs up to date on their shots, and the particular training you wish to perform with them. Do not forget to include information about how you intend on socializing your dogs to ensure that they are prime examples of the manner in which your dogs ought to be.

You will wish to make certain that you offer ample information in your breeding strategy so that you can review the strategy at a later date and respond to any concerns that you may have about the manner in which your breeding program ought to be working.

There are some things that you need to include in your breeding strategy so that you know you are going to achieve success at breeding.

1. The type of dogs you are going to possess

2. The number of dogs you believe you would have the ability to manage

3. Where your dogs are going to remain, and what kind of lodgings you are going to provide them

4. The veterinarian you are going to use

5. The quantity of cash you need to invest in dog care, veterinarian care, and all of the expenditures, and where that cash will originate from.

6. The number of years you intend on breeding dogs

7. Whether you intend on continuing your breeding program with dogs that you breed yourself, or whether you intend on introducing brand-new dogs to continue your program

8. What you are going to do with dogs when they can no more breed for you.

9. How you are going to handle problems in pregnancy and with pups that do not make it.

10. How you are going to understand when you can breed your dogs once again

11. How you will understand when it is time to quit.

12. Your general objective for breeding-- the kinds of things that you are trying to find in the breed and the kinds of things that you intend to attain by breeding the dogs that you have actually selected.

If you have the ability to have a breeding strategy that consists of these things, you'll discover that you have far more information at hand than you believed, and you'll have the ability to make an excellent choice about breeding dogs in general.

Keep in mind, you wish to have a breeding strategy that you can alter as you please, and one that is going to enable you to make a great decision about the kinds of dogs that you are going to be breeding. It is necessary to have the appropriate kind of breeding plan for your requirements, and it is really essential to ensure that you can follow through with your breeding strategy.

Likewise, your strategy should not be set in stone. There may be things that you wish to alter about your breeding strategy as time goes on, and you need to have the ability to quickly alter these things. It is going to be necessary for you to be versatile as a dog breeder so that you can make great choices about what is appropriate for you and for your dog.

Chapter 3: Exploring and Learning Breed Standards

In order to do a breeding strategy in the proper way, something that you are going to need to do is to establish an idea about the breed requirements that you are looking at and how to apply them to your personal dogs.

Taking a look at breeding requirements is a really essential method for you to make certain that you have a responsible breeding program. All of the breeds that exist that are either UKC certified or AKC certified are going to have breed requirements that have actually been established.

The requirements have actually been established for each breed by the individuals who register them and who have actually bred them for several years. For that reason, these are the requirements that are going to be necessary to you when it concerns ensuring that you have actually been doing the appropriate things in your program.

If you can not discover UKC or AKC breeding requirements for your dogs, you may want to search in other locations for the breeding requirements. There ought to be information from the UKC and AKC for those kinds of dogs. If you are going to be breeding a kind of dog that does not have either

UKC or AKC requirements, you need to search for the associations for that type that you can discover in your home nation. The associations are going to assist you in discovering the breeding requirements.

When you have the breeding requirements, you want to study them thoroughly. It is going to be essential for you to ensure that you understand precisely what kinds of things that you must be trying to find when it pertains to the dogs that you are going to be breeding.

The breed requirements will refer to the physical qualities that you are going to be trying to find, which are necessary to the breed. This may consist of a particular color scheme, and a particular idea about the particular markings that the dogs must have. It likewise ought to consist of the ways in which you are going to be taking a look at things such as ear shape, eye shape, and even colors of eyes and coat length.

The breed requirements will likewise include ideas about gait-- which is to state, how dogs that conform properly to that breed walk and move their body.

Breed requirements will have both things that you need to be searching for when you are breeding the dogs that you wish to keep in the breed, and things that you are searching for when you are breeding that you wish to maintain out of the breed. You need to be trying to find all of these things when you concentrate on the breeding requirements, since this is going to assist you in ensuring that you are breeding properly.

Get a copy of the breed requirements and study it, well before you actually bring home your breeding stock. This is going to assist you in making certain that you understand what you are trying to find.

Chapter 4: Getting Your Starting Stock

Your starting stock is going to be essential for you to get after you have actually chosen what you wish to breed, and after you have actually looked into the breeding requirements that you are going to be searching for.

Equipped with a copy of the breeding requirements, go to work looking for breeding stock for your own breeding operation. Keep in mind, nevertheless, that in some cases you want to modify what you are trying to find.

The most effective method to acquire breeding stock is to do so with pups. Naturally, this indicates that you are going to want to wait for a long period of time to begin breeding yourself, however you will have the most effective breeding stock that is possible. Try to find breeders that have great credibility among your own breed of dogs, and ensure that these are the kinds of breeders you are going to be collaborating with.

Then, look for a male and a female to begin with. It is never ever a great idea to begin a breeding program by getting more than two pups. You are going to wish to begin small, regardless of what you wish to carry out in the future. Locate a male and a female from 2 different breeders, or from the identical breeder if you can be sure that they are unrelated.

Take a look at the pedigrees of the pups before you purchase them. You are going to wish to make certain that there are no common relatives within a specific amount of generations. For several dog breeds that are little and brand-new, you may discover common relatives as far back as three or four generations, which might be great for that breed. Nevertheless, for breeds that have actually been around for a long period of time, you are going to wish to make certain that there are no common relatives for lots of generations.

Once again, a look at the breed requirements will assist you in determining what kinds of pedigrees you must be searching for in your pups. You ought to understand that ancestors that have championships are going to produce excellent pups, for the most part, and you will have the ability to be positive in understanding that you have actually gotten a starting stock that has champion bloodlines.

You must be taking a look at the pedigrees of the pups before you buy them. Then, make certain to follow all of that specific breeder's policies about the dogs and ensure that you have actually been authorized to own them. Purchase the pups, and bring them home.

You now have the beginnings of your breeding stock. Keep in mind, nevertheless, that you have simply begun on a journey that is going to be a lengthy journey certainly. It is going to be necessary that you follow through with your breeding strategy and the breeding requirements that you have looked into so that you can be certain you are offering your pups with the most effective home possible.

There are some things that you wish to try to find in your breeding stock.

1. Personality.

2. The quality of the dog.

3. The family tree of the dog.

4. Whether the dog has actually been shown. (in case you aren't purchasing a puppy).

5. If shown, what kind of championships the dog has actually gotten.

6. The mom and dad of the dog-- their personalities.

7. Where the pups are raised for the initial 8 weeks of their life.

8. What the breeder's requirements are all about, and what the objective of their company is all about.

9. What kind of training the mom and dad have actually had.

10. What kind of circumstance the young puppy was born in.

11. What the puppy appears like-- their markings and their colors.

12. If the puppy is welcoming.

13. If the puppy is going to enable you to turn him on his back and scratch his tummy while you hold him in your arms-- this reveals trust for individuals and love.

14. What size the pup is in contrast to his litter mates-- you need to select one that is not the largest nor the tiniest.

15. How the pup behaves with his littermates-- you need to pick a pup that is excellent with the other dogs which enjoys being with the other dogs. Do not select one that does not have fun with the other pups.

If you pick your breeding stock based upon these things, you ought to have the ability to have excellent breeding stock that you can depend upon.

Chapter 5: Raising Your Breeding Dogs

Now you have your starting stock, you are going to have the ability to begin on the breeding journey. However, initially, you get to do the enjoyable part, which is to raise pups from the beginning.

The very best breeding stock is going to be dogs that have actually been hand-raised by you from puppyhood. This will enable you to socialize the dogs correctly and to make sure that they are kept in such a way that you would be pleased to have them produce young puppies.

Do all of the routine things that you would be performing for pups while you are raising your breeding stock. Make certain that they are properly socialized, both with one another and with other animals, and individuals too. Take your pups out into the world and ensure that they meet other dogs, other animals and a great deal of individuals.

You may likewise wish to do training with your pups throughout this time. The more that you work with your breeding stock as long as they are young, the more likely they are going to be to generate top quality and healthy dogs for you down the road. Make certain that they are potty trained and that they understand all of the fundamental commands.

The most essential thing that you wish to do with your breeding stock is to make certain that they are properly socialized and that they are hand raised. These are both really crucial things due to the fact that they are going to assist you in seeing that you need to have dogs that are well-bred and effectively socialized. This is going to be your primary objective when it pertains to raising dogs.

Dogs that are hand-raised are going to be much better about the pups that they generate. They are going to produce high quality young puppies and they are going to enable you to help in the delivery process as you should. For that reason, you are going to wish to make sure that you are hand-raising your pups all the way to the adult years.

With some pure-blooded dogs, personality is the greatest problem that breeders look out for. For that reason, something that you are going to wish to do for sure is to ensure that you have actually produced a scenario in which the dogs are effectively socialized. This is specifically crucial if you are breeding a dog that is known to be capricious. You are going to wish to make a difference with your dogs.

Likewise, remember your breeding requirements and your breeding strategy. What is crucial to you about the breed of dogs and what do you wish to achieve? You need to have already selected a significant objective for your operation. Maybe it might be to produce pups that have a line that is known for being properly socialized, or maybe it may be to produce a line that is known for being high quality show dog.

No matter what your primary objective is, raise your young puppies with that in mind. The more that you are able to establish whatever it is that you are trying to find within them, the more that you are going to have the ability to know you have a high quality breeding program.

Chapter 6: Choosing When To Breed

When you are raising dogs to breed them, you are going to want to determine when you need to start the breeding procedure. This is really essential since you do not wish to breed a dog when they are too young, and you additionally do not wish to wait too long.

There are some great guidelines to follow when you are choosing when to breed your dogs. To start with, remember that you need to be ready for your dogs not to breed as you would like them to. Even if you have a male and a female does not indicate that they are going to breed properly, and it does not imply that they'll produce the puppies that you want them to.

A great guideline to follow is that you must never ever breed a female dog on her very first heat cycle, and not even on her 2nd if you can do something about it. You ought to wait till she is at least a year and a half old, or on her 2nd heat cycle, whichever precedes. A lot of breeders wait until the female is 2 years of age to begin breeding.

Male dogs are able to breed the moment they are at least a year old, although they may not develop completely before then, so you wish to watch on your male and ensure that he is the appropriate age.

Keep in mind in case you have a male and a female dog that are living together, you will want to keep them apart throughout the heat cycles that you do not want them to breed in. Your dogs are going to breed in case they get the opportunity, since dogs do not understand that they are too young, and they will not understand if they have actually already been bred on their last heat cycle. For that reason, it depends on you to make certain that breeding just happens when you want it to occur.

The first thing to consider is the age. Then, it is essential to think of how frequently. Responsible breeders will not breed their dogs on back to back heat cycles. So, in case your female dog has actually had a litter of pups on one cycle, even if she had no issues and the litter achieved success, you do not wish to breed her on the next one. Make certain that she is kept away from the male dog up until you are prepared to breed her once again.

Chapter 7: Developing Questionnaires and Waiting Lists

A responsible breeder is going to have a questionnaire for prospective owners, and is going to likewise have a waiting list for them. This assists you to supply yourself with an excellent idea of what owners are going to be like and it enables you to approve them even before you have pups.

If you have not currently done so, as you are waiting for your breeding stock to develop and be prepared for breeding, it is a great time to establish a website that you can utilize to discover houses for your pups. On the page, you need to have information about who you are and what you are going to achieve through breeding. You must additionally have a questionnaire.

This needs to be a series of questions that you are going to ask a prospective owner to complete. This is necessary to do, since you are going to wish to put your puppies in an excellent home, not simply the home that is going to pay the most for them. For that reason, something that you want to do is make questions that prospective owners will complete. Remember, if somebody does not wish to put in the time to complete the questionnaire about what sort of home they would offer, they aren't going to put in the time to offer your puppy with excellent home, either.

There are some fantastic questions that you ought to ask in your questionnaire, so that you know for certain what kind of home your pup is going to have. Here are a few sample questions to get you started.

What is your private information?

What kind of home do you have for your brand-new pup?

What do you wish to obtain from your brand-new pup?

Have you checked out the breed requirements?

What kinds of things are necessary for your pup to have?

Do you prefer a male or female?

Do you intend on breeding your pup?

Do you intend on showing your puppy?

Where is your puppy going to sleep?

What food will your puppy consume?

Who is going to be responsible for looking after your pup?

What kind of life will your brand-new young puppy have?

Will your puppy have a space in your house that is only for them?

Will your pup get ample exercise?

Do you have kids or do you plan to have them?

Will you instruct your kids about the obligations of having a dog?

Will you ensure that your kids treat your pup properly?

What will you do with your pup while you are at work?

Do you possess a fenced-in area for your young puppy to run in?

What kind of workout will your puppy get?

What kind of training are you going to have for your brand-new pup?

What is going to occur to your pup if you are no longer in a position to look after him?

Do you intend on adhering to the breed requirements for raising your puppy?

What dogs have you owned previously, and have you been happy with the breeds?

Which dogs were you not pleased with and for what reason?

Why do you wish to own one of our pups?

What will you provide to your brand-new puppy?

Providing a list of questions to your brand-new owners is going to let them understand what kind of home you expect the brand-new pup to have. This is going to be essential since it will help you see what kind of individuals are applying to own your pup. If they answer the questions and send the answers back to you, you understand that they are going to be responsible due to the fact that they have actually made the effort to fill out the answers to the questions. You can additionally get a great idea of the kind of home that they are going to offer and after that you can approve them.

When you have the questionnaire, you can start to enable individuals to fill it out and put them on waiting lists for your pups. These ought to be lists that you are going to call every now and then. When you have a litter of pups, you can enable individuals on the waiting list to have an initial pick at the pups.

Chapter 8: Breeding Itself

When you have everything established, you can start to really do the breeding procedure for your pups.

Once again, ensure that the dogs you are breeding are the appropriate age. You wish to make certain that you have waited for the correct amount of time, and that the dogs you are breeding are going to be at the top shape for breeding.

Take your female and your male dog to the veterinarian and ensure that they are prepared to be bred. Have them checked out, and make certain that they are in the appropriate health to breed. Get them up to date on their shots to ensure that you understand you are going to be breeding dogs that are in good shape and will not have any shot issues to stress over.

Then, you can allow nature to work its magic. Your female dog is going to enter into the season about two times a year. This is going to be different depending upon the breed. You are going to know that she is heading into the season since there is going to be a discharge that is visible from her. Anywhere from 5 to 10 days after you see the discharge, the male dog is going to have an interest in her. The majority of the time, male dogs are interested in the female well before she has an interest in them, so do not be dissuaded if it does not occur as quickly as you wish it to take place. Just enable your dogs to be alone together, and when the time is appropriate, they'll take care of business.

The majority of breeders do not do any helping when it pertains to the actual breeding. Nevertheless, with some tinier breeds, or with females that require support, some slight support, like holding the female in place, is needed. You are going to want to experiment and see if your dogs require any help, or if they are prepared to breed immediately.

As soon as your dogs have actually bred, you will want to treat your female as if she is pregnant. For the initial four weeks, keep her on her routine diet plan, however make certain that she has access to food any time she is starving. Do not get her too fired up and enable her to do what she wishes to do. Keep exercising her, nevertheless.

For the subsequent eight weeks, switch your pregnant dog to puppy food. This is going to assist her in getting the appropriate nutrients. Do not do this prior to the fifth week, nevertheless, as her body has to produce a number of things at the beginning of her pregnancy to be healthy-- and as pup food may not enable this to take place.

Let your mom dog do what she wishes to do, and remember that she may be moody or more caring than common. Keep her with you and keep her working out too. This is really essential to the excellent development of young puppies.

Chapter 9: Birthing Puppies

When it comes time to deliver your pups, there are a couple of things that you must understand so that your pups can be pleased and healthy and that your mom dog is going to be safe.

Firstly, keep an eye on the due date. Your veterinarian can assist you with this and, therefore, can provide you with information concerning your particular type.

As the due date comes closer, make certain that you are collecting your supplies. Your mom's dog must have a birth box that she can go to. Ensure that this remains in the area where you want your young puppies to be born. It ought to remain in an area that you frequently enter, such as your bedroom-- and if feasible, it ought to remain in the location where your mom dog sleeps during the night. This will enable her to be cozy with the puppies.

As it gets nearer, assemble a birthing set for yourself.

Tidy rags

Gloves

Iodine

Scissors

Eyedropper

Infant nose and mouth cleaner

q-tips

a scale

Make certain that the mom is cozy in her birth box and after that, wait.

When the time gets close, you'll have the ability to tell. Your mom dog is going to spend more time nesting in her box. As she enters into labor, she'll typically sit up and pant. You'll manage to see the contractions that she is having within her body.

Move her to the birth box and after that wait with her. The majority of mom dogs do not like to have puppies alone if they have great relationships with their owners.

As the pups start to be born, you are going to need to choose whether you wish to help. The majority of the time, nature can take its course, and the mom is going to deliver the young puppies.

If the mom is laboring for more than an hour after you have observed the sac and the puppy has actually begun to be born, you are going to wish to call a veterinarian to assist you. The pup might be stuck. Alternatively, you can carefully guide the puppy out by pulling lightly but strongly with a soft and wet rag. Attempt not to break the sac open as the puppy is still within the mom dog. If the sac does break, you'll want to get the pup out immediately.

When the pup is out of the mom, she needs to burst the sac and lick the pup's face. If she does not do this in a matter of seconds, you can burst the sac utilizing your fingernails or scissors.

Present the pup's face to the mom and get her to lick it tidy. You ought to hear the pup begin to breathe. In case the mom does not lick the puppies face, you may want to clean it for her and clear the puppy's nose and throat. You can perform this by utilizing the rag or the infant cleaner. The majority of

37

the time, the mom is going to clear the passages so the child can breathe.

In between pups, the mom needs to tidy up the majority of the mess and needs to clean up the little one. Attempt not to get in her way except if she is having issues with something. You can place the pup onto a nipple while she accomplishes this. Healthy puppies should wish to suck immediately.

The majority of pups are going to be born within a couple of hours of one another. If the mom dog is laboring and it has actually been more than a handful of hours in between pups, you must call a veterinarian since there could be something wrong.

As soon as all of the puppies have actually been born and the mom is no longer laboring, you are able to weigh the puppies and change the bed linen in the box. The mom is going to wish to go outdoors to go to the restroom, most likely. When she returns, make sure that you place the pups onto the nipples to eat.

Your primary objective must be to help the mom if she requires it. Look at them every now and then. It is always an excellent idea to move pups nearer to the mom in case they have actually been moved, and to put them on a nipple to ensure that they can eat.

There are some things to keep an eye out for immediately when it concerns pups. You must look for veterinarian's assistance instantly if:

A puppy does not eat

A pup isn't walking around

A puppy is being pressed sideways by the mom

A puppy is loud.

Healthy puppies need to:

Stay mainly peaceful

Put on weight every day

Be proactively eating

Breathe at a regular rate

Seem content.

Chapter 10: Raising Puppies

For the following eight weeks, you are going to be in charge of making certain that the pups are raised properly. It is going to be your role to make certain that the pups you are providing are effectively socialized and in good shape.

To start with, they ought to be taken to the veterinarian at some point after they are born. Nevertheless, you wish to make certain that they do not get too cold or too hot, so ensure that this isn't immediately. For an initial couple of days, leave them with their mom and attempt not to trouble them excessively.

Nevertheless, you must deal with the puppies. A mom dog that understands you and that trusts you is going to enable you to get the puppies, to weigh them regularly, and to pet them. You want the puppies to mature being used to being held and you want them to acknowledge you right from the beginning.

Grownups ought to deal with the young puppies after they are born. Don't take them out of the mom's view, and do not keep them any longer than she is able to stand. If she begins to get worried, put the pups back. Nevertheless, be there with them and her frequently, so that she is able to get used to you and so that she is able to get used to another person managing the puppies. This is really essential if you wish to make certain that the puppies mature well socialized.

Continue to deal with the puppies and to weigh them daily. Ensure that they are putting on weight, and if a puppy is not, look for the guidance of your veterinarian immediately. When they are a couple of weeks old they need to go to the veterinarian simply to ensure that they are healthy.

The puppies are going to be blind and deaf for a number of days after they are delivered. They ought to start to hear you within a couple of days, and ought to open their eyes in about a week. Puppies are going to grow really rapidly, and are going to look different from one day to the following.

The most effective thing that you are able to do for the puppies is to ensure that you are present, that you are holding them on a daily basis, and that the mom has great food, clear water, and lots of exercise and love. This is the most effective method to ensure that the family is in good condition.

As the pups grow older, they are going to open their eyes and start to be capable of walking. This is a great time to begin to present them to other individuals.

Due to the fact that you are going to be discovering homes for the puppies, make certain that you are socializing them to every little thing. To socialize a puppy to a thing have them experience it.

Keep them in an area with a television or radio on.

Have a ringing phone close by.

Have kids hold them

Have grownups hold them.

Enable them to walk and dash on various materials

Speak in loud voices and peaceful ones

Ensure they engage with the mom dog and with other dogs that you may have.

There are some things, nevertheless, that you ought to not allow your brand-new puppies to carry out.

Do not expose them to dogs aside from your own up until they have had their puppy shots.

Do not take them to the dog park up until they have actually had puppy shots.

Do not allow folks to handle them unless they have actually cleaned their hands.

Do not allow the pups to get extremely cold or extremely hot.

Maintain them out of drafts and far from windows.

Do not get them excessively thrilled.

Do not keep them far from their mom for more than a couple of minutes while they are nursing.

Do not allow them to consume anything besides puppy food when they are too young.

Raising puppies for the initial 8 weeks could be intriguing and time-consuming. There are a couple of things that you are going to want to be sure that you begin to do for the puppies so that you could be sure you are supplying the folks who purchase your puppies with an excellent dog.

Get them socialized to a collar and leash.

Take them for brief walks.

Begin to focus on potty training.

Get them consuming canned and firm puppy food, after their teeth appear, around 6 weeks.

Socialize, socialize, socialize!

Then, your puppies must be prepared for their brand-new homes!

Chapter 11: Waiting Lists and Interviews For Homes.

As soon as you understand how many puppies you have, and whether they are male or female, you are going to have some choices to make regarding what you wish to do with the pups. Often, you may wish to keep one for yourself. Numerous breeders are going to keep a female that they believe is good for their program, and after that, bring in a brand-new male, later on, to carry on their program. You additionally may wish to keep one for reasons aside from breeding.

When you understand what dogs you aren't keeping, you are able to begin to go through your waiting list to observe what kinds of homes are going to be offered for your pups. It is necessary for you to understand how you are going to be providing puppies to your waiting list-- is it a first come, first serve scenario, or do you have additional methods of matching puppies with homes?

After you understand which folks on your waiting list are going to have the ability to have the pups, you'll want to call them and tell them what you have, and see if they are curious. This is a great time to have them arrive at your house so you can meet them and they can choose the pup that they wish to have.

Keep in mind, just because somebody is on your waiting list does not indicate that they'll want a pup, and it additionally does not indicate that you owe them a pup. If somebody visits and you do not like them, trust them or do not like the manner in which they act around the puppy, there is no reason for you not to state that you aren't going to give them a puppy. Keep in mind, these are your puppies and your duty is to make certain that they go to the ideal houses possible. For that reason, do not hesitate to be choosy.

After you have actually approved of houses and folks have picked their puppies, you can request a deposit for holding that specific pup. Then, you can continue to raise the pup up until you feel that they are old enough to head to their brand-new homes.

Chapter 12: Providing Young Puppies With Brand-new Homes.

It is essential for you to ensure that the pups are old enough before you allow them to proceed to their brand-new homes. You wish to wait till they are at least 8 weeks old, but additionally up until they are completely weaned. Some breeds require longer, and some breeders love to have the pups remain longer so that they can be certain they are in good shape.

Regardless of what you choose for yourself, it is necessary to continue to instruct and socialize the dog as long as they are with you. By 8 or 10 weeks old, a pup needs to be having a great idea of what it means to go potty outdoors, and ought to be eating by themselves. Then, you can feel free to have them proceed to their brand-new homes. Simply ensure that you feel prepared and that you believe the puppies are prepared.

Bear in mind that in some cases the mom dog has things to teach the puppies even after they have actually been weaned, so you may wish to wait for this to take place.

Chapter 13: Contracts.

It is constantly going to be necessary to have contracts when you are handling pups. You wish to ensure that you have a great owner contract that you are able to refer to, which is going to lay out what the brand-new owner needs to be doing with your dog. You may include things like a puppy back system, where if the brand-new owner breeds the dogs, you can get a pup back if that is what you decide.

Additionally, you may wish to think about a clause that states that the puppy ought to be returned to you if the brand-new owner can't maintain it. This is going to assist you to be responsible. Keep in mind that this isn't simply a product that an individual is purchasing from you, it is a life-- so you want to ensure that your contract explains this and that your contract is done properly.

There are numerous things to feature in puppy contracts.

What occurs if an owner can't maintain the dog?

Can the dog be shown?

Does the dog have to be neutered/spayed?

How should the dog be managed?

Can the dog be kept outdoors or does it have to live indoors?

Just how much does the pup cost?

Is the breeder liable for anything throughout the puppy's lifespan?

Producing a contract can allow you to make certain that you have ample information and can provide you the assurance that you require to assure yourself that the puppy is going to be properly looked after.

The agreement needs to be signed by all of the parties that are included, and you wish to make sure that you are notarizing the contract. Keep in mind that no matter how good the deal may appear to be, there may be issues that develop, so a contract is constantly a great idea, no matter what.

Checking Up on Puppies

Something else that you are going to wish to do with your puppies is to constantly check up on them. Lots of contracts consist of declarations that the new owners need to offer the breeders with images or information for a specific period of time. This is done for lots of reasons. It enables you to keep control over the pups, and it enables you to make certain that you take responsibility and that they have actually headed to a great home. It additionally enables you to be in command of making certain that the contract is being followed.

Chapter 14: Understanding The Truth

As soon as you have actually gone through a litter of pups and gotten them off to great houses, you may be interested in knowing when it is going to be time to breed once again. It is really essential for you to ensure that you understand what you are doing. Do not breed dogs on her subsequent heat cycle after she has had a litter of puppies. You may wish to wait a year or more, depending upon how tough the pregnancy and litter was on the mom dog. These are all choices that you must make when you are breeding dogs to ensure that you can be certain you are offering good quality pups.

Understanding When To Not Breed

Part of being a responsible owner is understanding additionally when not to breed your dogs. You do not wish to breed a dog prematurely, but you additionally may want to decide not to breed the dog if she had a tough pregnancy, had a tough litter, or had issues weaning or looking after the pups. A responsible breeder is going to understand when not to breed once again.

What To Breed For

There are numerous things that you wish to breed for. When you are taking a look at the dogs that you want to breed, and when you are making judgments about those dogs and choosing which ones to breed, you need to try to find a number of things.

Personality-- how the dog behaves around you, around other folks, and around other animals or kids.

Physical state:

Colors

Size

Ear Shape

Eye Shape and Color

Coat Density

Gait

Health

Long life expectancy

Less of a possibility of illness

In case your dog has these qualities as required in the breed requirements, you may wish to think about breeding them.

What To Breed Out

There are likewise numerous things that you are going to wish to breed out. This indicates that if you have a dog that displays these things, you'll wish to neuter or sterilize them and put them in a pet quality home.

Illness

Flimsy Joints or Knees

Coats that are not appropriate for breed requirements

Inappropriate Gait

Colors or markings that do not comply with breed requirements

Incorrectly shaped ears, eyes, or facial attributes

Bad personality

Propensity towards shyness

If your dog has these things, you may wish to think about not breeding them, so you do not pass on the characteristics that you do not wish to pass on.

Chapter 15: Showing Dogs

You may choose that you wish to show dogs. This is something that numerous breeders do and that is necessary for a great deal of various breeding programs. If you choose that you wish to show dogs, there are a couple of things to bear in mind.

To start with, showing dogs can be a great deal of work. You are going to want to be sure that you have the appropriate types and information so that you can get registered for the show early enough. You'll additionally want to be sure that you are prepared to show dogs, implying that you have had the appropriate time to work with your dogs.

When you are figuring out whether to show dogs, there are several questions that you must ask yourself so that you understand you are showing the appropriate kinds of dogs.

Does your dog comply with breed requirements?

Is your dog properly trained or can you train him/her quickly to walk within the ring?

Is your dog cozy with somebody touching him/her and raising her up?

Is your dog cozy with other dogs?

Will your dog bite or will he/she attempt to trouble the other animals?

Are you prepared to take a trip to shows with your dog?

Is a dog showing anything you believe you would like as a pastime?

The answers to these questions are going to aid you to ensure that you have actually offered ample information about your dog and that you understand your dog is going to be great in the ring. This is something that you are going to wish to think thoroughly about before you show your dog.

Showing a dog can result in excellent things for your dog. He/she is going to have the ability to be much better trained, and as you undergo more shows he/she'll discover much more. Additionally, you'll have the ability to manage your dog better.

Having championships, or having accreditations from being shown is an essential thing in the breeding world. Sometimes individuals will wish to have your puppies if the parents have actually been shown since it reveals that your dogs are fantastic examples of the kind of dog that they are searching for.

Concluding Chapter: Lifetime Breeding And Ownership

It is essential to keep in mind that owning a dog implies you are going to have a lifetime of breeding and ownership duties. In case you are breeding dogs, you are going to want to understand that you are responsible for that dog, and you are additionally responsible for the puppies that originate from the dog. This suggests that as a responsible breeder, one of the most crucial things that you can carry out is to ensure that you supply your puppies with an assurance.

As a breeder, you must be prepared and happy to reclaim any puppies that the brand-new owners can not keep. This implies that you want to be happy to be responsible for any puppies that you offer, regardless of the length of time you are in business for and regardless of the length of time you breed puppies or how many you breed. This is going to assist you to ensure that you are breeding properly.

Likewise, you want to bear in mind that as soon as you have actually bought a dog, even with the purpose of breeding him or her, you are responsible for that dog. If the dog does not match breed requirements and can not breed, or if the dog can not breed for any other reason, you are nonetheless responsible for that dog for the dog's whole life. For that reason, you may wind up owning dogs that do not breed. When a dog is done breeding for his/her life, you are still responsible for possessing that dog, and you want to bear in mind this to ensure that you could be a responsible dog owner.

I hope that you enjoyed reading through this book and that you have found it useful. If you want to share your thoughts on this book, you can do so by leaving a review on the Amazon page. Have a great rest of the day.

Made in the USA
Las Vegas, NV
11 January 2021